Karl Darbyshire, Geoffrey Waterworth, David Charles Webb

A Web-Based Approach to Evaluate and Enhance Pump Performance Using Embedded Optimisation

Pump Optimisation

GRIN Verlag

Bibliografische Information der Deutschen Nationalbibliothek:

Die Deutsche Bibliothek verzeichnet diese Publikation in der Deutschen National-
bibliografie; detaillierte bibliografische Daten sind im Internet über http://dnb.d-
nb.de/ abrufbar.

Imprint:

Copyright © 2011 GRIN Verlag GmbH
Druck und Bindung: Books on Demand GmbH, Norderstedt Germany
ISBN: 978-3-640-85134-8

This book at GRIN:

http://www.grin.com/en/e-book/168187/a-web-based-approach-to-evaluate-and-
enhance-pump-performance-using-embedded

GRIN - Your knowledge has value

Der GRIN Verlag publiziert seit 1998 wissenschaftliche Arbeiten von Studenten, Hochschullehrern und anderen Akademikern als eBook und gedrucktes Buch. Die Verlagswebsite www.grin.com ist die ideale Plattform zur Veröffentlichung von Hausarbeiten, Abschlussarbeiten, wissenschaftlichen Aufsätzen, Dissertationen und Fachbüchern.

Visit us on the internet:

http://www.grin.com/

http://www.facebook.com/grincom

http://www.twitter.com/grin_com

A Web-Based Approach to Evaluate and Enhance Pump Performance Using Embedded Optimisation

K J Darbyshire, G Waterworth, D Webb

Leeds Metropolitan University, Faculty of Arts, Environment and Technology, Headingley Campus, Leeds, LS6 3QS, England, UK.

Abstract

Selection and configuration are widely met tasks in design; this is an example of a web-based selection/configuration tool with embedded optimisation. Pumps inevitably deteriorate over their product lifecycle, in which interaction generally occurs in terms of flow, pressure and electricity consumption. Practical implementations of pump scheduling suggest that a 10% of the annual expenditure on energy costs may be saved. The object is to minimise the energy cost incurred, while selecting the best schedule of legal available pumps. The results illustrate that the recording of pump characteristics over the internet provides an efficient method of pump performance and evaluation.

Introduction

This paper describes the development of a secure web-based database that gives support to hydraulic engineers enabling them to select cost efficient pump combinations over the Internet Throughout the water industry, many methodologies of cost management have been adopted to enable the reduction of significant energy costs. Methods such as the refurbishment of deteriorated pumps, the use of high efficient motors, employing the most efficient pumps and ensuring that water is pumped using the smallest hydraulic head will enable substantial savings. The techniques of optimal scheduling are relevant to many areas of manufacturing and production engineering, such as scheduling of material flow, production planning, tool and plant scheduling, job shop scheduling and single machine scheduling. Optimal scheduling will effectively reduce the average job response. time, thus improving system efficiency and cost reduction. Using the combined methods of pump modelling, factorial analysis, linear programming and the Internet technologies, will provide an efficient process to enable the monitoring of pump performance and evaluation.

General Description and Methodology

Figure 1 illustrates a typical high-lift water pumping station (WPS) that consists of five fix speed water pumps connected in a parallel configuration. Each pump extracts clean water from a close by water supply tank and provides the customer with clean water via a water storage tank. The pumps are operated over a twenty-four hour period and individually monitored using micro-controller processors (MCP). The MCP's enable the parameters of pump flow, pressure and energy consumption, on the delivery side of the pumps, to be recorded (Darbyshire & Waterworth. 2004). Figure 2 illustrates the total power consumption produced by the pumps over a twenty-four hour period.

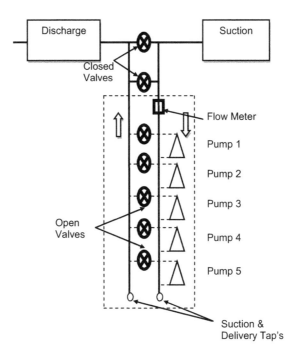

Figure 1: Water Supply System Schematic

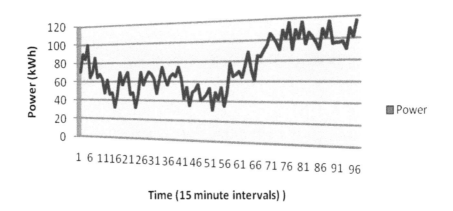

Figure 2: Total Pump Power Consumption

Figure 3 illustrates how the logged data is transmitted to the 'pump control room' through an outstation, commonly known as a remote telemetry unit (RTU) (Reynolds. 2004). The hydraulic engineer may then analyze

the data and enable the construction of pump characteristic models and cost effective schedules to improve system efficiency.

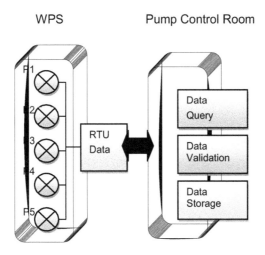

Figure 3: Data Transfer between WPS and Pump Operator

Since the WPS consist of five high-lift pumps, there are 32 (2^5) possible pump combinations during each two hourly switch over. The cost of generating electricity is more economical throughout the night than during the expensive daytime period. Due to this nightly rebate, optimum pumping is more cost effective through the hours of 1800hrs to 2400hrs (Darbyshire & Waterworth 2003). The electricity tariff for nightly use is 1.2p per hour, where the more expensive day period i.e. 0000hrs to 1800hrs is 2.86p per hour. The cost function for the applied problem is illustrated as follows:

$$Cost = \sum_{t=1}^{24} \sum_{n=1}^{5} fn_{(t)} Pn.Rn$$

(1)

Where:

R=Tariff

P=Power (kWh)

Q=Flow

D=Demand

X=Reservior Level

f=On/Off

t=Time(hrs)

n=Pump Number

T=Total

Other constraints for the optimisation model are that the maximum discharge capacity of the WPS must not exceed 2500m^3 and the minimum must not fall below 1250m^3 as illustrated below:-

$$Level_{(T)} = \left(\sum_{t=1}^{T} \sum_{n=1}^{5} fn_{(t)} Qn \right) - D_{(t)}$$

(2)

While constrained to the maximun and minimum limits:

$$x_{max} > \sum_{t=1}^{24} \sum_{n=1}^{5} fn_{(t)} Qn_{(t)}$$

(3)

$$x_{min} < \sum_{t=1}^{24} \sum_{n=1}^{5} fn_{(t)} Qn_{(t)}$$

(4)

Web Technologies

Over the last decade, the use of the Internet has been used broadly to circulate information globally. Due to the rise of Web 2.0 technologies such as e-commerce, online learning and online resources etc, there is the increased need for server side applications. Using the existing technologies of Hypertext Mark-Up Language (HTML), Java Server Pages (JSP) and Server Query Language (SQL), with a secure web based server, power, flow and pressure produced by the individual pumps may be monitored over the Internet (Lee & Scheeman. 2000). JSP enables the use of static HTML content with server side scripting to produce a dynamic output and is implemented as a classic three-tier client/server as illustrated in Figure 4.

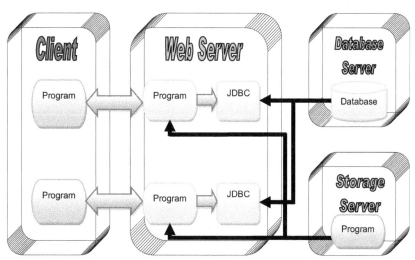

Figure 4: Client / Server: Three-Tier Architecture

The Java Database Connectivity (JDBC) Application-Programming Interface (API) allows the hydraulic engineer situated in the control room to interact with the SQL database server. Using Microsoft Excel and Direct Data Access (DDA), pump characteristics may be displayed in the form of a spreadsheet. The information may then be used to construct pump models using Matlab[®], to calculate their best efficiency point (BEP) of operation as illustrated in Figure 5. A pump is then selected so that it runs at its best efficiency BEP relating to the expected system curve at the pumps BEP (Bunn. 2009). This is achieved using the pump affinity laws to help derive maximum flow, power and pump efficiency.

$$MaxFlow = \frac{Q}{Q_{max}} = \left(1 - \frac{H}{H_{cut}}\right)^{\frac{1}{c}}$$

(5)

$$MaxHead = \frac{H}{H_{cut}} = 1 - \left(\frac{Q}{Q_{max}}\right)^{c}$$

(6)

$$H_{syst} = \frac{H_{stat} + Q^2}{h_f}$$

(7)

$$Efficiency = \frac{Q.H.SpGr}{P}$$

(8)

Where:

H = Head

H_{cut} = Head is at zero

H_{syst} = System Head Curve

H_{stat} = Static Head Component

Q_{max} = Maximum Flow

h_f = Valve and Pipe Losses

c = Pump Manufactures Coefficients

SpGr = Specific Gravity

The pump models are verified against the pump manufactures characteristics to identify any problems as illustrated in Figure 6. The graph illustrates the manufactures bench test curve, for the efficiency of a pump, against the live conditions of a currently monitored pump. By comparing the two curves, it is evident that at BEP the pump has deteriorated by 8.5%

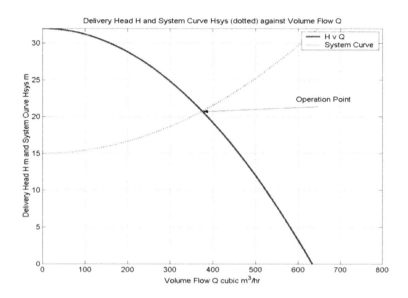

Figure 5: Best Efficiency Point of Pump Modelled in Matlab®

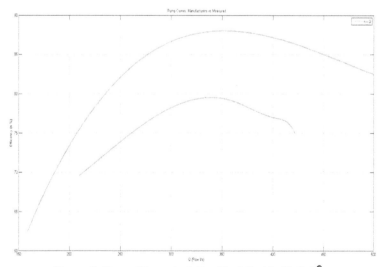

Figure 6: Pump Characteristics Modelled in Matlab®

Power Conservation

Pumps operating in combinational sequences show evidence of interaction, in which certain configurations prove more efficient than the sum of each running alone. If there is evidence of interaction between pumps, then the data may be used to construct a comprehensive scheduling package using this additional information. The implementation of fractional analysis enables important pump information to be established by the extraction of interactive data from the database (Darbyshire & Waterworth. 2004). This is a statistical technique used to

simultaneously analyse data considering several factors in an experiment (Montgomery. 2009). Figure 7 depicts a screen shot of the Matlab® command window illustrating which of the pumps are significant to the experiment.

The Matlab® simulation has been verified by using the statistical f-distribution tables to identify the observed significance of each pump under test.

$$F_0 > F_{\alpha 1,10(n-1)}$$

(9)

At the significance level of α=0.05 the critical value for Pump 1, from the statistical f- distribution table, is 5.32. Hence, the significance limits for pump number one are:

$$F_0 > F_{\alpha 1,10(n-1)} = 95.888, p < 0.05$$

(10)

$$F_0 > F_{(1,10)0.05} = 4.96$$

(11)

```
Command Window                                                    _|□|×|
File  Edit  Debug  Desktop  Window  Help                              »
① New to MATLAB? Watch this Video, see Demos, or read Getting Started.  ×

South Milford Pumping Station ANOVA for Pump Power Consumption Over 24hrs

    PUMP          SUM        DEGREES      MEAN        F       P         PUMP
 COMBINATIONS    SQUARES     FREEDOM    SQUARES    RATIO    RATIO   SIGNIFICANCE

 Pump  1        1870.563        1       1870.563  95.865    0.000        *
 Pump  3         390.063        1        390.063  19.990    0.001        *
 Pump  1&3      1314.063        1       1314.063  67.345    0.000        *
 Pump  4         855.563        1        855.563  43.847    0.000        *
 Pump  1&4      1105.563        1       1105.563  56.659    0.000        *

 Model         5535.813
 Error          195.125       10        19.512
 Total         5730.938       15

 R Squared = 96.595    Radj Squared = 94.893
>>
```

Figure 7: Pump Significance Modelled in Matlab®

By implementing a normal probability plot of effects as illustrated in Figure 8, pump interaction is more evident. The plot shows that they are no middle point pump effects that follow a normal distribution. This concludes that the pump effects and interactions have a significant effect on the experiment. The normal probability plot also clearly illustrates that the two-way interaction of Pumps 1 and 3 have a negative effect on the response and with the aid of optimal scheduling a significant cost reduction for power consumption may be achieved.

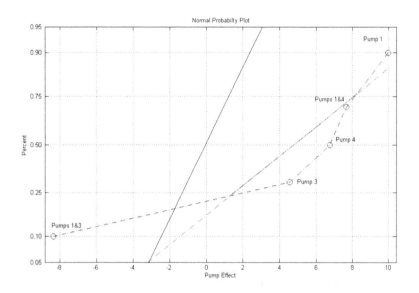

Figure 8: Matlab® Normal Probability of Pump Effects

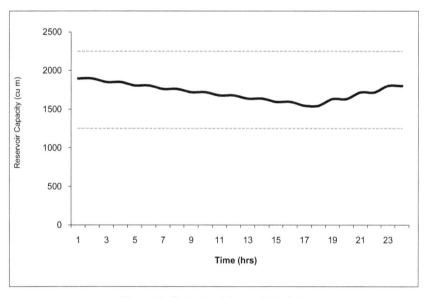

Figure 9: Optimised Pump Schedule

Pump Optimisation

The fundamental aim of optimisation is to minimise or maximise a cost function, which is a measure of the performance of some aspect of the process under consideration (Chen & Coulbeck. 1991). This paper uses the mathematical technique of Linear Programming (LP) to calculate an optimum policy using a sequence of decisions (Bryds & Ulanicki. 1994). There are many optimisation techniques that have been previously implemented such as Dynamic Programming (DP), Genetic Algorithms (GA's), Simulated Annealing (SA) (Darbyshire & Waterworth. 2001). Linear programming has been implemented in this paper due its short computational time taken to find an optimum solution. LP implements a systematic approach to calculate a

minimum objective in the terms of linear equations (Levin & Lamone. 1969). The time taken to run the algorithm depends on the required accuracy of the results. For a WPS incorporating five pumps the algorithm takes less than thirty seconds to compute. Figure 9 illustrates the optimised pumping schedule adhering to the system constraints discussed earlier in this paper.

Summary and Conclusions

Selection and configuration are widely met tasks in design. This paper has successfully illustrated an example of a web-based selection/configuration tool with embedded optimisation. The results demonstrate a cost effective method of pump performance and evaluation over the Internet. Due to implementing the combined methodologies of Internet technologies, linear programming and factorial analysis an effective and accurate process of secure pump asset management has been implemented.

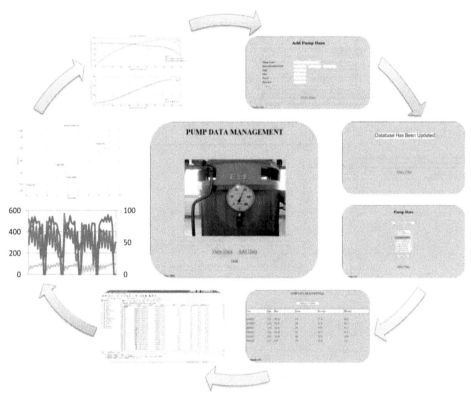

Figure 10: Pump Performance and Evaluation Over the Internet

The results illustrate that the web server may be remotely accessed, which enables hydraulic engineers to compare pump manufactures data to identify deterioration or any irregularities in the water distribution system. The pump characteristics have been modelled in Matlab®, which calculates the pumps best efficiency point using the resistance system curve of the water system. Factorial analysis and subsequent optimal scheduling enables a significant cost reduction. Figure 10 illustrate the product development cycle of pump performance and evaluation over the Internet. The full extent of this knowledge management system is illustrated in Figure 11. This aspect will bring potential savings in manpower cost due to the system being operated according to

scenarios generated by the pump asset management system rather than a hydraulic engineer. Ultimately, the tasks required to enable such a system are pump data collection, monitoring the results of the pump conditions and raising alarm either audible, an email or short message service (SMS) (Mustard & Harrison)(Karnachi, Waterworth & Darbyshire. 2004).

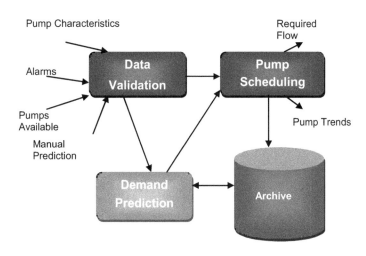

Figure 11: Pump Asset Management System

References

Bunn, S. (2009) Operating Pumps to Maximise Efficiency. Pump & Pipelines. Water. June 2009.

Bryds, M. A., Ulanicki, B. (1994) Operational Control of Water Systems: Structures, Algorithms and Applications. Prentice Hall.

Chen, Y. C., Coulbeck, B. (1991) Optimized Operation of Water Supply Systems Containing a Mixture of Fixed and Variable Speed Pumps. International Conference on Control 91, pp 1200-1205.

Darbyshire, K, J., Waterworth, G. (2001) Comparison of Methods of Pump Scheduling in Water Supply Systems. European Simulation and Modelling Conference, ESM2001, ENGIN-28 Prague, June 2001.

Darbyshire, K, J., Waterworth, G. (2003) Optimal Scheduling Utilizing Factorial Analysis and Constrained Optimisation. The International Journal for Manufacturing Science & Production. Advances in Manufacturing Research in the UK. Selected Papers from the 18th National Conference on Manufacturing Research National Conference on Manufacturing Research in the UK, Guest Editors by Cheng, K., Webb, D. Vol 5, NOS 1-2, 2003, Freud Publishing House Limited.

Darbyshire, K, J., Waterworth, G. (2004) Pump Asset Operation and Performance Monitoring over the Internet. Advances in e-Engineering and Digital Enterprise Technology. Fourth International Conference on e-Engineering

and Digital Enterprise Technology (e-ENGDET). Edited by Cheng, K., Webb, D. and Marsh, R. Professional Engineering Publishing Limited.

Reynolds, L. (2004) Developments in Control in the Water Industry. IEE Computing and Control Engineering. February/March 2004. Pages 39-43.

Karnachi, N, A., Waterworth, G., Darbyshire, K, J. (2004) Assessment of the Possibility to Remotely Monitor and Control a pH Process – An Experimental Study. Advances in e-Engineering and Digital Enterprise Technology. Fourth International Conference on e-Engineering and Digital Enterprise Technology (e-ENGDET). Edited by Cheng, K., Webb, D. and Marsh, R. Professional Engineering Publishing Limited.

Lee, K, B., Scheeman, R, D. (2000) Distributed Measurement and Control Based on the IEEE 1451 Smart Transducer Interface Standards. IEEE Transactions on Instrumentation and Measurement. Vol 49, No 3, June.

Levin, R., Lamone, R. (1969) Linear Programming for Management Decisions. Richard, D. Irwin Inc, Homewood, Illinois.

Montgomery, D, C. (2009) Design and Analysis of Experiments: International Student Version. Seventh Edition, John Wiley & Sons (Asia) Pte Ltd.

Mustard, S., Harrison, S. (2004) Future Requirements for Remote Telemetry Units. IEE Computing and Control Engineering. February/March 2004. Pages 45-47.

Authors Information and Interests

Mr Karl James Darbyshire was born in Barnsley, South Yorkshire England and started his career as an electrical electronic engineer. In 1994, he studied for his first degree at Sheffield Hallam University and obtained a BSc_{HONS} in Electronic Information Technology. In 1997, he progressed and completed a master's degree at the University of Huddersfield in MSc Electronic Computer Based Systems Design. After completion, he decided to travel around the world for sixteen months, enjoying the opportunity to broaden his outlook and develop interests in other countries. On return, he was employed as a part time lecturer at Leeds Metropolitan University within the Faculty of Information and Engineering Systems, School of Engineering and achieved the Post Graduate Certificate in Research Methodology. In Karl's spare time, he enjoys outdoor activities from fell scrambling to rambling and take pleasure from performing and watching motorsport activities and events. Currently he is a part of the research group at the Leeds Metropolitan University and has registered for PhD General Engineering the 'Investigation of Optimal Pump Scheduling, Pump Model Identification and Prediction Techniques'. He has published numerous conference proceedings and journals relative to this area of research.

http://repository.leedsmet.ac.uk/main/search.php?q=darbyshire&SearchGroup=Research

Mr. Geoffrey Waterworth began his career in 1964 as a control engineer with British Aerospace in Stevenage and progressed to Ferranti, the electronic defence corporation, and then the semiconductors giant SGS Fairchild. In 1978, he became Senior Lecturer at Leeds Metropolitan University and supervised an extensive

range of research projects in the areas of pump optimisation, modern adaptive control techniques and sensor fault detection in water quality monitoring. Geoff has written numerous books and has published his work in the form of technical papers. In his spare time, he enjoys ice climbing, mountaineering, and mountain travel and is a member of the British Alpine Club. Since retiring from Leeds Metropolitan University he has undertook his passion for water colour and mix media painting and become the exhibition secretary and organiser of the Harrogate and Nidderdale Art Club. http://www.handnart.co.uk/html/aboutUs.asp

Prof. David Charles Webb achieved his DPhil in the subject area of Space Physics from the University of York in 1975. After three years as a post-doctoral researcher at the University of York in conjunction with Bell Laboratories, he undertook the position of Directorate of Scientific and Technical Intelligence at the Ministry of Defence in London. In 1979 he moved to the Computer Unit at Leeds Metropolitan University and then to the Faculty of Information and Engineering Systems, School of Engineering in the early 1980's. Dave has published extensive scientific articles relating to the application of engineering modelling and on the subject matter of nuclear disarmament and the militarisation of space, in which he was the cofounder of the Praxis Centre, which comprises a multidisciplinary research group that investigates the aspects of information technology, technology in peace, conflict resolution and human rights, within today's existing society. He is currently the Professor of Engineering Modelling, Head of the Centre for Applied Research in Engineering and the Associate Director of the Praxis Centre at Leeds Metropolitan University. http://praxis.leedsmet.ac.uk/praxis/